BECOMING A DISCIPLE

DISCOVERING

GOD'S WILL.

SERENDIPITY
HOUSE

GROUP DIRECTORY

Pass this Directory around and have your Group Members
fill in their names and phone numbers

Name   Phone

_____   _____

_____   _____

_____   _____

_____   _____

_____   _____

_____   _____

_____   _____

_____   _____

_____   _____

_____   _____

_____   _____

_____   _____

_____   _____

_____   _____

BECOMING A DISCIPLE

Discovering God's Will.

EDITING AND PRODUCTION TEAM:

James F. Couch, Jr., Lyman Coleman, Sharon Penington, Cathy Tardif,
Christopher Werner, Matthew Lockhart, Richard Peace, Erika Tiepel,
Andrew Sloan, Katharine Harris, Gregory C, Benoit,
Margaret Harris, Scott Lee

SERENDIPITY
HOUSE

NASHVILLE, TENNESSEE

Published by Serendipity House Publishers
Nashville, Tennessee

International Standard Book Number: 1-57494-306-5

ACKNOWLEDGMENTS

Scripture quotations are taken from the Holman Christian Standard Bible,
© Copyright 2000 by Holman Bible Publishers. Used by permission.

03 04 05 06 07 08 / 10 9 8 7 6 5 4 3 2

Nashville, Tennessee
1-800-525-9563
www.serendipityhouse.com

TABLE OF CONTENTS

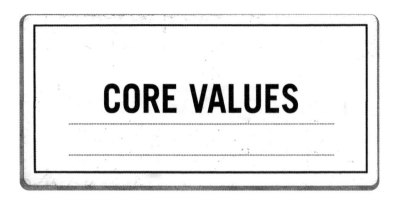

CORE VALUES

Community: The purpose of this curriculum is to build community within the body of believers around Jesus Christ.

Group Process: To build community, the curriculum must be designed to take a group through a step-by-step process of sharing your story with one another.

Interactive Bible Study: To share your "story," the approach to Scripture in the curriculum needs to be open-ended and right brain—to "level the playing field" and encourage everyone to share.

Developmental Stages: To provide a healthy program throughout the four stages of the life cycle of a group, the curriculum needs to offer courses on three levels of commitment: (1) Beginner Level—low-level entry, high structure, to level the playing field; (2) Growth Level—deeper Bible study, flexible structure, to encourage group accountability; (3) Discipleship Level—in-depth Bible study, open structure, to move the group into high gear.

Target Audiences: To build community throughout the culture of the church, the curriculum needs to be flexible, adaptable and transferable into the structure of the average church.

Mission: To expand the kingdom of God one person at a time by filling the "empty chair." (We add an extra chair to each group session to remind us of our mission.)

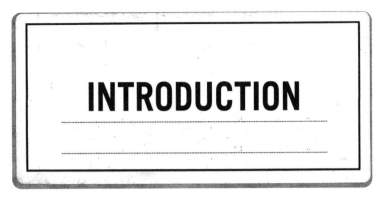

INTRODUCTION

EACH HEALTHY SMALL GROUP WILL MOVE THROUGH VARIOUS STAGES AS IT MATURES.

MULTIPLY STAGE: The group begins the multiplication process. Members pray about their involvement in new groups. The "new" groups begin the life cycle again with the Birth Stage.

BIRTH STAGE: This is the time in which group members form relationships and begin to develop community. The group will spend more time in ice-breaker exercises, relational Bible study and covenant building.

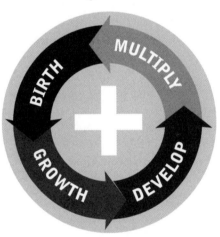

DEVELOP STAGE: The inductive Bible study deepens while the group members discover and develop gifts and skills. The group explores ways to invite their neighbors and coworkers to group meetings.

GROWTH STAGE: Here the group begins to care for one another as it learns to apply what they learn through Bible study, worship and prayer.

SUBGROUPING: If you have nine or more people at a meeting, Serendipity recommends you divide into subgroups of 3–6 for the Bible study. Ask one person to be the leader of each subgroup and to follow the directions for the Bible study. After 30 minutes, the Group Leader will call "time" and ask all subgroups to come together for the Caring Time.

EACH GROUP MEETING SHOULD INCLUDE ALL PARTS OF THE "THREE-PART AGENDA."

 Ice-Breaker: Fun, history-giving questions are designed to warm the group and to build understanding about the other group members. You can choose to use all of the Ice-Breaker questions, especially if there is a new group member that will need help in feeling comfortable with the group.

One of the purposes of this book is to multiply this group into a new groups. Therefore, getting to know one another and discover the talents and spiritual gifts of others in the group is essential to the success of this course. The goal is to learn more about one another.

 Bible Study: The heart of each meeting is the reading and examination of the Bible. The questions are open, discover questions that lead to further inquiry. Reference notes are provided to give everyone a "level playing field." The emphasis is on understanding what the Bible says and applying the truth to real life. The questions for each session build. There is always at least one "going deeper" question provided. You should always leave time for the last of the "questions for interaction." Should you choose, you can use the optional "going deeper" question to satisfy the desire for the challenging questions in groups that have been together for a while.

It is important for the group to learn how to better facilitate relational Bible Study. There are no right or wrong answers to the questions. The group members should strive to make all of the other group members feel comfortable during the Bible Study time. Because, we all have differing levels of biblical knowledge, it is essential that we appreciate the personal context from which answers are given. We should also look for those who have natural abilities to make others at easy in sharing. To begin new groups it is important to identify and train new facilitators and leaders.

 Caring Time: All study should point us to actions. Each session ends with prayer and direction in caring for the needs of the group members. You can choose between several questions. You should always pray for the "empty chair." Who do you know that could fill that void in your group?

For this group to multiply it is important to bring new people into the group. As the group grows and new leaders are trained, multiplication will become natural. Each week it is important to remember to pray for those who God would fill your empty chair. As God brings new people into your life, remember to ask them to join your group. This might be the start of a whole new adventure for someone. God will increase your group and add to the kingdom at the same time.

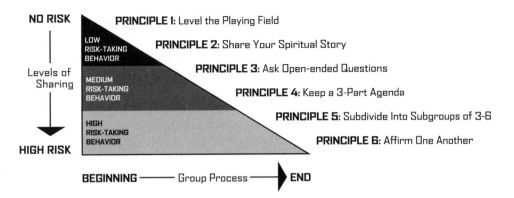

Sharing Your Story: These sessions are designed for members to share a little of their personal lives each time. Through a number of special techniques, each member is encouraged to move from low risk, less personal sharing to higher risk responses. This helps develop the sense of community and facilitates caregiving.

Group Covenant: A group covenant is a "contract" that spells out your expectations and the ground rules for your group. It's very important that your group discuss these issues—preferably as part of the first session.

GROUND RULES:

- *Priority:* While you are in the group, you give the group meeting priority.
- *Participation:* Everyone participates and no one dominates.
- *Respect:* Everyone is given the right to their own opinion and all questions are encouraged and respected.
- *Confidentiality:* Anything that is said in the meeting is never repeated outside the meeting.
- *Empty Chair:* The group stays open to new people at every meeting.
- *Support:* Permission is given to call upon each other in time of need—even in the middle of the night.
- *Advice Giving:* Unsolicited advice is not allowed.
- *Mission:* We agree to do everything in our power to start a new group as our mission.

GOALS:

- The time and place this group is going to meet is_____.

- Refreshments are _____ responsibility.

- Child care is _____ responsibility.

- This group will meet until _____ at which time we will decide to split into new groups or continue our sessions together.

- Our primary purpose for meeting is _____.

TEN STEPS FOR MULTIPLYING SMALL GROUPS

1. **Share a vision:** From the very first meeting of a group the vision must be cast for the mission. God can greatly affect the larger body of Christ through a small group if there is a vision for creating new groups and bringing people into the kingdom. If the group will make a group covenant that envisions multiplying into new groups, then new groups will happen. An effective leader will regularly keep this goal in front of the group. It is essential to raise up group leaders from your group and to divide into new groups every 18–24 months. Announce the intention to multiply early and often.

2. **Build a new leadership team:** As the group matures through the Growth and Develop Stages, the present leadership team should identify apprentice leaders and facilitators. This is done best in a small group setting. Look for an engineer type as the group administrator, the party animal as the hospitality person, a person that loves interaction and knowledge as the facilitator and a caring person to handle group shepherding. Next you must seek to train and mentor them as they grow in confidence. Here is an outline of this process:

   a. Identify apprentice leaders and facilitators
   b. Provide on-the-job training
   c. Give them the opportunity to lead your group
   d. Introduce the new team to your church
   e. Launch the new group

3. **Determine the type of group:** Who are you trying to reach? Here are four commonly identified audiences.

Group		Percentage	Group Type
a.	Core	10%	Discipleship Group
b.	Congregation	30%	Pulpit or Care Groups
c.	Crowd	60%	Felt Need Groups
d.	Seekers	Outsiders	Support Groups
e.		All	Affinity Groups
f.		All	Covenant Groups

4. **Conduct a Felt Need Survey:** Use either a custom survey for your church or the one included in this book to determine an area or a specific topic for your first study.

5. **Choose curriculum:** Make sure your choice fits the group type and the stage in the life cycle of your group. All Serendipity courses are pre-selected for stage of the life cycle.

6. **Ask someone to serve as host:** Determine when and where the group will meet. Someone must coordinate the following.

   a. Where the meeting will be held.
   b. Who will provide babysitters (if necessary).
   c. Who will teach children (if necessary).
   d. Who will provide refreshments.

7. **Find out who will go with the new team:** There are several options in beginning new groups.

    a. Encourage several members of your group to go with the new leadership team to start a new group.
    b. The existing leadership team will leave to start a new group leaving the existing group with the new team.
    c. Several groups can break off beginning all new groups.

8. **Begin countdown:** Use a study designed to help multiply groups, building each week until you launch your new group.

9. **Celebrate:** Have a party with presents for the new group. Make announcements to your church, advertising the new group and its leadership team.

10. **Keep casting a vision:** Remember as you start new groups to keep casting a vision for multiplying into new groups.

LEADERSHIP TEAM FOR SMALL GROUPS

Coordinator: Is responsible to the church leadership team for:
1. Building a leadership team.
2. Ensuring the coordination of the group.
3. Meeting with the leadership team once a month for encouragement and planning.
4. Casting a vision for multiplication and beginning the process of multiplication.

Facilitating Team: Is responsible to the coordinator for:
1. Guiding the group in life-changing Bible study.
2. Developing a facilitating team for subgrouping into groups of three to six.
3. Keeping the group on agenda, but being sensitive when someone needs to share.
4. Subdividing the group for Bible study and caring time and emphasizing the "empty chair."

Care Team: Is responsible to the coordinator for:
1. Contacting group members to encourage attendance and personal growth.
2. Keeping the group informed of prayer needs.
3. Coordinating caring for the special needs of the group.

Party Team: Is responsible to the coordinator for:
1. Planning, coordinating and promoting monthly group parties.
2. Keeping the members involved in the party activities.

Host/Hostess: Is responsible to the coordinator for:
1. Providing a clean home with enough space to subdivide into groups of three to six.
2. Coordinating refreshments.
3. Welcoming guests and having name tags at each meeting.
4. Making sure everything is conducive for sharing (no TV, comfortable temperature, arrangements for children).

FELT NEED SURVEY

Rank the following factors in order of importance to you with 1 being the highest and 5 being the lowest:

_____ The passage of Scripture that is being studied.

_____ The topic or issue that is being discussed.

_____ The affinity of group members (age, vocation, interest).

_____ The mission of the group (service projects, evangelism, starting groups).

_____ Personal encouragement.

Rank the following spiritual development needs in order of interest to you with 1 being the highest and 5 being the lowest:

_____ Learning how to become a follower of Christ.

_____ Gaining a basic understanding of the truths of the faith.

_____ Improving my disciplines of devotion, prayer, reading Scripture.

_____ Gaining a better knowledge of what is in the Bible.

_____ Applying the truths of Scripture to my life.

Of the various studies below, check the appropriate circles that indicate: if you would be interested in studying for your personal needs (P), you think would be helpful for your group (G), or you have friends that are not in the group that would come to a study of this subject (F).

	P	G	F
Growing in Christ Series (7-week studies)			
Keeping Your Cool: Dealing With Stress	O	O	O
Personal Audit: Assessing Your Life	O	O	O
Seasons of Growth: Stages of Marriage	O	O	O
Checking Your Moral Compass: Personal Morals	O	O	O
Women of Faith (8 weeks)	O	O	O
Men of Faith	O	O	O
Becoming a Disciple (7-week studies)			
Discovering God's Will	O	O	O
Time for a Checkup	O	O	O
Learning to Love	O	O	O
Foundations of the Faith (7-week studies)			
Knowing Jesus	O	O	O
Foundational Truths	O	O	O
Understanding the Savior (13-week studies)			
Mark 1–8: Jesus, the Early Years	O	O	O
Mark 8–16: Jesus, the Final Days	O	O	O
John 1–11: God in the Flesh	O	O	O

	P	**G**	**F**
John 12–21: The Passion of the Son	○	○	○
The Miracles of Jesus	○	○	○
The Life of Christ	○	○	○
The Parables of Jesus	○	○	○
The Sermon on the Mount: Jesus, the Teacher	○	○	○

The Message of Paul

	P	**G**	**F**
Romans 1–7: Who We Really Are (13 weeks)	○	○	○
Romans 8–16: Being a Part of God's Plan (13 weeks)	○	○	○
1 Corinthians: Taking on Tough Issues (13 weeks)	○	○	○
Galatians: Living by Grace (13 weeks)	○	○	○
Ephesians: Together in Christ (12 weeks)	○	○	○
Philippians: Running the Race (7 weeks)	○	○	○

Words of Faith

	P	**G**	**F**
Acts 1–14: The Church on Fire (13 weeks)	○	○	○
Acts 15–28: The Irrepressible Witness (13 weeks)	○	○	○
Hebrews: Jesus Through the Eyes of Hebrew Faith (13 weeks)	○	○	○
James: Faith at Work (12 weeks)	○	○	○
1 Peter: Staying the Course (10 weeks)	○	○	○
1 John: Walking in the Light (11 weeks)	○	○	○
Revelation 1–12: End of Time (13 weeks)	○	○	○
Revelation 13–22: The New Jerusalem (13 weeks)	○	○	○

301 Bible Studies with Homework Assignments (13-week studies)

	P	**G**	**F**
Ephesians: Our Riches in Christ	○	○	○
James: Walking the Talk	○	○	○
Life of Christ: Behold the Man	○	○	○
Miracles: Signs and Wonders	○	○	○
Parables: Virtual Reality	○	○	○
Philippians: Joy Under Stress	○	○	○
Sermon on the Mount: Examining Your Life	○	○	○
1 John: The Test of Faith	○	○	○

Felt Need Series (7-week studies)

	P	**G**	**F**
Stress Management: Finding the Balance	○	○	○
12 Steps: The Path to Wholeness	○	○	○
Divorce Recovery: Picking Up the Pieces	○	○	○
Parenting Adolescents: Easing the Way to Adulthood	○	○	○
Blended Families: Yours, Mine, Ours	○	○	○
Dealing with Grief and Loss: Hope in the Midst of Pain	○	○	○
Healthy Relationships: Living Within Defined Boundaries	○	○	○
Marriage Enrichment: Making a Good Marriage Better	○	○	○

SESSION 1

CALLED TO BE A DISCIPLE

SCRIPTURE: Luke 5:1–11

Welcome to this course on discovering God's will! Together we will explore the topic of our "gifts and calling" and be encouraged as we see God's unique design for our lives and learn how we can serve him better.

Our gifts and calling are central elements of our uniqueness as people. Our gifts are the specific, Spirit-given abilities that enable us to contribute to the wider good of the community and world. Our calling is the task or area of service where God directs us to use those gifts. Our calling is sometimes called our "vocation," though at times that word is too closely identified with a paid job. Our calling may or may not be the same thing as our paid job. Sometimes a calling is something we need to do as a volunteer.

It can be difficult for many of us to determine our calling. How do we know what God is calling us to do? Some people have a strong sense of this in high school; others do not discover it until well into adulthood. Former tennis great Arthur Ashe (who died in 1993) was looking for his vocation after his tennis career was over, and even after he contracted AIDS from a blood transfusion. He wrote in his book *Days of Grace*: "If God hadn't put me on this earth mainly to stroke tennis balls, he certainly hadn't put me here to be greedy. I wanted to make a difference, however small, in the world, and I wanted to do so in a useful and honorable way."

The focus of this course is to help us search together for how we can:

- Hear God's call.
- Discover our gifts.
- Develop those gifts.
- Take risks.
- Put the future into God's hands.
- Have a servant mind.

We want to open our minds and hearts to hear God's voice as we study the Scripture passages and share our own stories. Together we will help each other to discover God's will for our lives.

Every session in this course has three parts: (1) **Ice-Breaker**—to get to know each other better and introduce the topic; (2) **Bible Study**—to share your life through a passage of Scripture, and (3) **Caring Time**—to share prayer concerns and pray for one another.

ICE-BREAKER
Connect with your Group | **15 Min.**

Today we are beginning our journey together by talking about the first step in God's calling: the call to follow Jesus. Take some time to get to know each other by sharing your responses to the following questions.

1. What is the strangest or the most unpleasant job you have ever had to do?

2. How many career changes have you made in your life? What prompted those changes?

3. In what areas of your life are you more likely to try something new, and in what areas do you resist change?
    - ○ Clothing.
    - ○ Hairstyle.
    - ○ Car.
    - ○ Church.
    - ○ Small group.
    - ○ Food.
    - ○ Where I live.
    - ○ What I do for a living.
    - ○ Making new friends.
    - ○ Other_____.

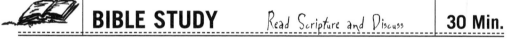

BIBLE STUDY
Read Scripture and Discuss | **30 Min.**

In this first session, you will have a chance to share about God's call in your life. This passage is from the beginning of Jesus' ministry and focuses on the calling of his first disciples. Read Luke 5:1-11 and notice the fishermen's response to Jesus' odd request.

Jesus Calls the First Disciples

Luke: **5** *As the crowd was pressing in on Jesus to hear God's word, He was standing by Lake Gennesaret. ²He saw two boats at the edge of the lake; the fishermen had left them and were washing their nets. ³He got into one of the boats, which belonged to Simon, and asked him to put out a little from the land. Then He sat down and was teaching the crowds from the boat. ⁴When He had finished speaking, He said to Simon,*

Jesus: *"Put out into deep water and let down your nets for a catch."*

Simon Peter:	⁵*"Master," Simon replied, "we've worked hard all night long and caught nothing! But at Your word, I'll let down the nets."*
Luke:	⁶*When they did this, they caught a great number of fish, and their nets began to tear. ⁷So they signaled to their partners in the other boat to come and help them; they came and filled both boats so full that they began to sink. ⁸When Simon Peter saw this, he fell at Jesus' knees and said,*
Simon Peter:	*"Depart from me, because I'm a sinful man, Lord!"*
Luke:	⁹*For he and all those with him were amazed at the catch of fish they took, ¹⁰and so were James and John, Zebedee's sons, who were Simon's partners.*
Jesus:	*"Don't be afraid," Jesus told Simon. "From now on you will be catching people!"*
Luke:	*"Then they brought the boats to land, left everything, and followed Him.*

Luke 5:1–11

 | # QUESTIONS FOR INTERACTION

***LEADER

Be sure to read the Summary and Study Notes at the end of this session and refer to these during the discussion as needed. If 30 minutes is not enough time to answer all of the questions in this section, conclude the Bible Study by answering question 7.

1. When did you first hear the "call" to begin your spiritual journey? Did you respond right away? Share with the group about the beginning of your faith journey.

2. In comparison to the fishermen, where are you right now in your spiritual journey?
   ○ Like Simon, ready to do what Jesus says even if I don't understand it.
   ○ Afraid of what might be ahead.
   ○ Seeing myself as unworthy to follow Jesus.
   ○ Sinking, like the boat full of fish—I'm getting too much all at once.
   ○ Dropping everything to follow him.
   ○ I'm not sure what he wants from me.
   ○ Other_____.

3. What is the tone in Simon's voice when he answers Jesus in verse 5? How would you paraphrase his comment?
   ○ Say what?
   ○ You think you know more about fishing than I do?
   ○ I think this is a waste, but I'm going to do this just because of who you are.
   ○ What do you know that I don't?
   ○ I would do anything to make up for a lost night of fishing.
   ○ There is no way I would go out right now, but if it is the only way to get my boat back I'll do it.
   ○ I value you so much that I'll put aside my own judgment.
   ○ Sure, there is nothing else to do until I go out tonight with the boat.
   ○ This should be worth a laugh.
   ○ Other _____.

4. What was Jesus' purpose in providing the miraculous catch of fish? How do you think this contributed to the disciples' willingness to follow? Did you experience any "sign" of who Jesus is at the beginning of your journey?

5. What is Jesus referring to when he says that the fishermen will be "catching people" (v. 10)? What would this look like in your life?

6. What does it mean today to leave everything and follow him (v. 11)? How close do you think you have come to doing this?

7. How would you characterize your follow-through on your call to be a disciple?
   ○ Jesus is my Lord, and I follow him daily.
   ○ Jesus is a great Teacher: I listen, but follow when I like.
   ○ Jesus is my Savior, but we don't have a close relationship.
   ○ Jesus is my Messiah, and I'm here to find out what that means.

GOING DEEPER: *If your group has time and/or wants a challenge, go on to this question.*

8. Why does Peter respond to the huge catch of fish the way he does in verse 8? Have you ever looked at yourself in this light? What did you see?

CARING TIME *Apply the Lesson & Pray for One another* | 15 Min.

This very important time is for developing and expressing your concern for each other as group members by praying for one another.

1. Agree on the group covenant found in the introductory pages.

2. Begin the prayer time by taking turns sharing a specific praise or problem.

3. Share any other prayer requests and then close in prayer. Pray specifically for God to bring someone into your group to fill the empty chair next week.

NEXT WEEK

Today we focused on Jesus' calling of his first disciples, and talked about our own responses to the call to follow God and be a disciple. In the coming week, thank God for his call in your life and ask him for wisdom as you seek to grow in your faith. Next week we will dig deeper into the subject of calling as we discuss how to differentiate between the voice of God and our own ideas.

Summary: All four of these fishermen had probably at least seen Jesus around and were familiar with who he was. When the crowd began to press too close, Jesus asked Simon to take him out a little way in his boat. Sound travels well over water, and this way the people in the back of the crowd had a better chance of hearing. Simon made no objection to lending his boat, but he couldn't help protesting when Jesus asked him to do a seemingly silly thing. Nevertheless, he agreed to do it anyway, and their fruitless night was suddenly recouped. It must have been startling to say the least. In the other gospel accounts, Jesus specifically says, "follow me," but Luke does not mention this. Instead, he focuses on Simon's realization of his own sinfulness and on Jesus' rather unusual response: "Don't be afraid ... from now on you will be catching people!"

5:1 Lake Gennesaret. This is another name for the Sea of Galilee.

5:2 washing their nets. In the morning, fishermen would clean and repair their nets that they dragged along behind the boats while fishing through the night.

5:3 the boats. While one belonged to Simon, the other boat may have been owned by James and John (Mark 1:19), Simon's partners in the fishing business (v. 10). These would have been open craft about 20 to 30 feet long.

5:4–5 From any normal perspective, Jesus' command was absolutely foolish since mid-morning was not the time fish would be feeding. To get the feeling behind the words in verse 5, one must picture tired and hungry men who have worked unsuccessfully all night suddenly wondering why in the world they should listen to a religious teacher when it comes to their fishing business! Still, Peter decides to go along with him and is rewarded for it.

5:6–7 In contrast to Simon's doubt, Luke underscores the magnitude of the catch. It was so large that it tore the nets and threatened to sink Simon's boat as well as that of his partners!

5:8 Peter's fear and confession before Jesus is similar to that of people in the Old Testament when they encountered the divine (1:12,29; 2:9; Isa. 6:5; Dan. 10:15). In particular, as with Isaiah, encountering divine power caused Peter to focus on his awareness of his own sinfulness. In Isaiah's case, God responded by sending an angel to "cleanse" him with a burning coal. Then, as with Peter, God gave Isaiah a mission (Isa. 6:8). Just what Peter recognized about Jesus' identity at this point is unclear since "Lord" can be a title for God or a title of respect for an esteemed person. In any case, it is apparent that Peter was thoroughly convinced that Jesus was at least a rabbi who was more interesting than most.

5:10 Don't be afraid. Jesus' words echo those of the divine response seen in Isaiah 6, Daniel 10 and elsewhere. **you**

will be catching people! The climax of the story is not Jesus' self-revelation, but its significance as a graphic illustration of the certain widespread success that would accompany Peter's (and the other apostles') mission of preaching the kingdom of God (4:43). While fish are caught to their own detriment and for the advantage of another (those who will eat them), people are "caught" for their own benefit—that they might realize the fullness of God's love and forgiveness.

5:11 they ... left everything, and followed Him. A loyalty to Jesus that takes precedence over anything else in life is Luke's characteristic way of describing what it means to be a follower of Christ.

SESSION 2

HEARING GOD'S CALL

SCRIPTURE: ACTS 16:6-10

In the session last week, we focused on God's call to follow him, and shared with one another the beginnings of our own spiritual journey. This week we will further explore the idea of "calling," as we discuss hearing God's voice amid the confusion of our world.

ICE-BREAKER

Connect with your Group

15 Min.

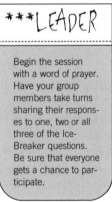

***LEADER

Begin the session with a word of prayer. Have your group members take turns sharing their responses to one, two or all three of the Ice-Breaker questions. Be sure that everyone gets a chance to participate.

We all know that half of hearing is listening, but sometimes we forget to do it. Take turns listening to each other now, as you share from your own life experiences.

1. Who in your family do you feel is the best listener when you want to talk?
   ○ My spouse.
   ○ My mom or dad.
   ○ The dog.
   ○ My sister or brother.
   ○ The wall.
   ○ A close friend who is like family.
   ○ Other_____.

2. Would you usually rather be the one talking or the one listening?

3. When has being willing to listen enabled you to hear something important that you would have been sorry to miss out on?
   ○ When one of my kids confided in me.
   ○ When someone asked me for help.
   ○ When my spouse was hurting, and I was able to help.
   ○ When God was able to penetrate my thick head.
   ○ When I was lonely and hurting and I found comfort.
   ○ When I was encouraged by someone else's story.
   ○ Other_____.

 **BIBLE STUDY** *Read Scripture and Discuss* | **30 Min.**

***LEADER**

Ask a member of the group, selected ahead of time, to read aloud the Scripture passage. Then divide into subgroups of three to six and discuss the Questions for Interaction.

This story occurred when the apostle Paul was on a missionary journey to establish new churches. Prior to this, all of the churches he had established had been in the area known as Asia Minor. This call led to the first churches in Europe. Read Acts 16:6-10 and notice the way this group was in tune to God's calling.

Called in a New Direction

⁶They went through the region of Phrygia and Galatia and were prevented by the Holy Spirit from speaking the message in the province of Asia. ⁷When they came to Mysia, they tried to go into Bithynia, but the Spirit of Jesus did not allow them. ⁸So, bypassing Mysia, they came down to Troas. ⁹During the night a vision appeared to Paul: a Macedonian man was standing and pleading with him, "Cross over to Macedonia and help us!" ¹⁰After he had seen the vision, we immediately made efforts to set out for Macedonia, concluding that God had called us to evangelize them.

Acts 16:6–10

 QUESTIONS FOR INTERACTION

***LEADER**

Refer to the Summary and Study Notes at the end of this session as needed. If 30 minutes is not enough time to answer all of the questions in this section, conclude the Bible Study by answering questions 6 and 7.

1. When was the last time you made a decision that changed the direction of your life and work?

2. How confident were you at the time that this decision was right?
    - ○ I thought I might be making a mistake, and I didn't know what to do.
    - ○ I felt funny about it.
    - ○ Not at all sure—I was just guessing.
    - ○ Rather unsure, but willing to take a chance.
    - ○ Confident, but realizing I could be wrong.
    - ○ Thought that this was the only thing I knew to do.
    - ○ Confident, knowing this was the right thing to do.
    - ○ I was excited and couldn't wait to get moving.
    - ○ Other _____.

3. If you had dreamed about the man in Macedonia, how would you have most likely reacted?
   ○ Figured it was something I ate.
   ○ Dismissed it as a dream.
   ○ Sought counseling.
   ○ Not told a soul.
   ○ Waited for confirmation.
   ○ Considered it a message from God.
   ○ Other_____.

4. What gave Paul such a strong sensitivity to the Holy Spirit's guidance?

5. What is the closest you have come to having a clear message from God, like Paul's vision?

6. What will you look for as you seek to determine whether your dreams or thoughts are God's call for your life or just your own ideas?
   ○ A vision in the night like Paul had at Troas.
   ○ Obstacles put in my way (like Paul at Bithynia).
   ○ A change in my thought pattern.
   ○ Consistent indications in my daily life.
   ○ The needs of others around me.
   ○ Consistency with the values and teachings of Scripture.
   ○ God will have to talk to me directly.
   ○ I will need confirmation from people I respect and trust.
   ○ Other_____.

7. What obstacles do you see ahead of you in your present life path? Are these obstacles just normal obstacles that come in life, or are they God's way of telling you to take another direction? How can you tell?

GOING DEEPER: *If your group has time and/or wants a challenge, go on to this question.*

8. Do you think that God has a specific direction for you in each situation in your life, or does discerning God's will have more to do with what your attitudes and moral character should be than with specific decisions?

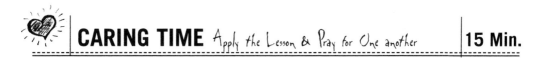

LEADER

Bring the group back together for the Caring Time. Begin by sharing responses to all three questions. Then share prayer requests and close in a group prayer. Those who do not feel comfortable praying out loud should not feel pressured to do so. As the leader, conclude the prayer time and be sure to pray for the empty chair.

This time of sharing and prayer is particularly important for the mutual encouragement of the group. Take turns responding to the following questions, and then pray for one another.

1. How sensitive do you feel you are to the Holy Spirit's leading?
   ○ I feel very connected.
   ○ I need powerful hearing aids.
   ○ I'm not sure I would know his voice if I heard it.
   ○ I don't know where to begin.
   ○ From time to time I feel very connected.
   ○ Most of the time I'm clueless.
   ○ I'm learning to stay tuned in.
   ○ Other_____.

2. What is something you feel God may be calling you to do?

3. In what specific situations can this group pray for you as you seek to follow God's leading in your life?

P.S. Add new group members to the Group Directory at the front of this book.

Today we saw a dramatic example from Paul's life of God's specific leading, and discussed the question of how we can discern God's call in our own lives. In the coming week, ask God to give you wisdom and discernment as you deal with the situations you mentioned in question 3 of the Caring Time. Next week we will be talking about discovering our spiritual gifts. Learning to use the gifts God has given us is integral to discovering and following his call.

NEXT WEEK

Summary: One of the most obvious facts about the work of the church in Acts is that the Holy Spirit was an integral part of all that happened. The Holy Spirit is referred to no less than 41 times in the book. Certainly most of us remember that the Holy Spirit filled the disciples at Pentecost (ch. 2). The Holy Spirit also helped Peter when he was hauled before the Sanhedrin (4:8); filled Stephen in his hour of martyrdom (7:55); healed Saul's (Paul's) blindness (9:17-19); brought increased numbers to the church (9:31); led Gentiles to become believers (10:44-48); set apart Paul and Barnabas for their missionary journeys (13:2); and prepared Paul for the suffering he would face (20:23).

In our passage for this week, the apostle Paul shows a special sensitivity to the Holy Spirit's leading, and as a result he is led to take the Gospel to Europe for the first time. How significant this is! It was in Europe that the Gospel grew and spread throughout the rest of the earth. Because it became the dominant faith in Europe, it came to America and became the dominant faith here as well.

The events of this chapter occur in what is called Paul's second missionary journey. The Holy Spirit led the missionary team, and that leading was away from Asia and Bithynia. In essence, they were told not to divert their path to the right or the left, but to go straight ahead, which would have been the direction of Europe. When they got to Troas, which is on the Aegean Sea across from Greece, Paul saw a vision at night. It was a man of Macedonia, calling them to "cross over and help us." Macedonia is part of Greece. Right away Paul knew that this was why they had been forbidden to go in the direction he had considered. He did not hesitate to follow what he believed to be the call of the Holy Spirit. Our text tells us "we immediately made efforts to set out for Macedonia" (v. 10).

16:6–7 the Holy Spirit / the Spirit of Jesus. Luke clearly identifies the ongoing work of Jesus with the agency of the Holy Spirit in the lives of the apostles.

16:7 did not allow them. Why Jesus would not allow Paul and Silas and Timothy to preach in Asia and Bithynia is not given. Later on, the apostle Peter was in contact with churches in that area, so they were not left bereft of the Gospel (1 Peter 1:1).

16:8 Troas. An important seaport on the Aegean Sea. While it appears Paul did not do any evangelistic work here at this time, he did do so later on (2 Cor. 2:12).

16:9 Macedonia. This area of northern Greece had been the dominant power under Alexander the Great in the fourth century B.C.

16:10 we. Verses 10–17 is the first of three passages in Acts written in the first person (20:5–21:18; 27:1–28:16), indicating that Luke himself was accompanying Paul at these points.

SESSION 3

DISCOVERING OUR GIFTS

SCRIPTURE: ROMANS 12:1-8

Last week we explored the question of how to discern God's calling as we try to make wise decisions. Today we will focus on the gifts God has bestowed upon all believers, and on discovering our own gifts and learning to use them.

ICE-BREAKER   Connect with your Group | 15 Min.

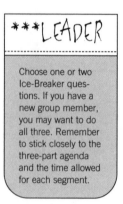

***LEADER**

Choose one or two Ice-Breaker questions. If you have a new group member, you may want to do all three. Remember to stick closely to the three-part agenda and the time allowed for each segment.

Every believer receives special gifts from God, to be used for the edification of the body and for the glorification of God. Before we go on to explore spiritual gifts in more depth, take some time to get to know one another better by sharing your answers to the following questions.

1. When you were a child, what was the most exciting gift you ever received? Who gave it to you?

2. What family traditions do you have for opening Christmas presents? Which do you think is more fun: watching other people open the gifts you chose for them, or opening your own?

3. Have you ever received a gift that you weren't too excited about at first, but that turned out to be really useful? What caused you to see this gift through different eyes?

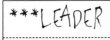

Integrally related to hearing God's call is discovering our gifts. There are differences of opinion among Christians about spiritual gifts—what they are, how they are received and how they should be used. But there is virtual agreement that God does give all believers spiritual gifts and that these gifts should be used for the edification of the church, God's glory and our fulfillment. Read Romans 12:1-8 and think about what your own gifts might be.

Living Sacrifice

Reader One: *12 Therefore, brothers, by the mercies of God, I urge you to present your bodies as a living sacrifice, holy and pleasing to God; this is your spiritual worship. ²Do not be conformed to this age, but be transformed by the renewing of your mind, so that you may discern what is the good, pleasing, and perfect will of God.*

Reader Two: *³For by the grace given to me, I tell everyone among you not to think of himself more highly than he should think. Instead, think sensibly, as God has distributed a measure of faith to each one. ⁴Now as we have many parts in one body, and all the parts do not have the same function, ⁵in the same way we who are many are one body in Christ and individually members of one another. ⁶According to the grace given to us, we have different gifts:*

Reader One: *If prophecy, use it according to the standard of faith;*

Reader Two: *⁷if service, in service;*

Reader One: *if teaching, in teaching;*

Reader Two: *⁸if exhorting, in exhortation;*

Reader One: *giving, with generosity;*

Reader Two: *leading, with diligence;*

Reader One: *showing mercy, with cheerfulness*

Romans 12:1–8

QUESTIONS FOR INTERACTION

***LEADER

Refer to the Summary and Study Notes at the end of this session as needed. If 30 minutes is not enough time to answer all of the questions in this section, conclude the Bible Study by answering question 8.

1. How many spiritual gifts do you think a person should expect to have?

   ○ The more the better.

   ○ Only one, and don't mess with the others.

   ○ One main gift and several other less dominant gifts.

   ○ I don't think it is possible for a person to know specifically what the gift is.

   ○ Other_____.

2. How does the implied responsibility of having a spiritual gift make you feel?

   ○ Scared.

   ○ Elated.

   ○ Tired.

   ○ A little apprehensive, but excited.

   ○ Other_____.

3. In the past week, did you feel more "conformed" or "transformed"? What is the difference?

4. What does it mean for you to offer your body as a living sacrifice to God (v. 1)?

5. How can you "renew your mind" (v. 2)? What is the result if you do so?

6. What would "thinking sensibly" about yourself look like? How is this connected to spiritual gifts? In what ways could you be thinking of yourself more highly than you ought?

7. Do you know anyone who seems to be really using his or her gift? In what ways does this person benefit the rest of the body?

8. Do you know what your gifts are? If not, how do you think you could discover them?

○ Ask God to reveal them to me.

○ Take an informal survey of what other believers perceive about me.

○ Take a spiritual analysis test.

○ Try working in every area and see where I seem to fit the best and accomplish the most.

○ Look back at what I have done in the past, and see where God has used me the most.

○ Other_____.

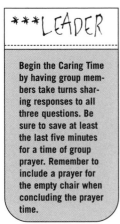 GOING DEEPER: *If your group has time and/or wants a challenge, go on to this question.*

9. What is the difference between a natural talent and a spiritual gift? How can you tell whether a gift is natural or spiritual? Is there any overlap? Does God give spiritual gifts to nonbelievers? (What about good teachers or leaders who are not believers?)

CARING TIME *Apply the Lesson & Pray for One another* | 15 Min.

***LEADER

Begin the Caring Time by having group members take turns sharing responses to all three questions. Be sure to save at least the last five minutes for a time of group prayer. Remember to include a prayer for the empty chair when concluding the prayer time.

The main purpose of the spiritual gifts is to minister to one another. Take this time to do just that as you share your responses to the following questions and pray for one another's needs.

1. Are you struggling with determining your gifts or calling? How can the group pray for you as you seek God?

2. How could you use the ministry of an exhorter/encourager in your life right now? How about a teacher or a leader or a servant?

3. Share any special requests or praises you would like the group to pray about.

In the lesson this week, we explored the subject of spiritual gifts and talked about how to discover our own gifts. During the coming week, consciously think about where God has used you in the past, and ask him to show you where you can be best used in the future. Thank him for giving you a special gift to use for his glory. Next week we will continue the study of spiritual gifts as we consider how to implement them in the body.

NOTES ON ROMANS 12:1–8

Summary: The first 11 chapters of the apostle Paul's letter to the Romans are known for their emphasis on doctrine and theology. With chapter 12, Paul shifts to practical teaching for how believers should live. Paul writes that one of the ways we can please God and strengthen the body of Christ is by knowing and using our spiritual gifts.

12:1 by the mercies of God. A Christian's motivation to obedience is overwhelming gratitude for God's mercy. **bodies.** The Christian lifestyle is not a matter of mystical spirituality that transcends one's bodily nature, but an everyday, practical exercise of love (6:13; 13:8). The idea of "bodies" also emphasizes the metaphor of sacrifice since one puts bodies on the altar. **sacrifice.** In the Old Testament sacrificial system, the victim of the sacrifice becomes wholly the property of God. Sacrifice becomes holy, i.e., set apart for God only. **living ... holy ... pleasing to God.** In Greek, these three phrases are attached with equal weight as qualifiers to "sacrifices." The idea is not that

God counts living sacrifices the same as the dead animals in the old system, but rather that he wants Christians to live in fullness of life, in accord with his principles (i.e., sanctification), and hence to be the kind of sacrifice desired by God.

12:2 Do not be conformed. Believers are no longer helpless victims of natural and supernatural forces that would shape them into a distorted pattern; rather they now have the ability to resist such powers. **be transformed.** The force of the verb is "continue to let yourself be transformed"; i.e., a continuous action by the Holy Spirit that goes on for a lifetime. A Christian's responsibility is to stay open to this process as the Spirit works to teach them to look at life from God's view of reality. **renewing of your mind.** Develop a spiritual sensitivity and perception—learn to look at life on the basis of God's view of reality. Paul emphasizes the need to develop understanding of God's ways. **discern.** Christians are called to a responsible freedom of choice and action, based on the inner renewing work of the Holy Spirit.

12:3–8 Paul now turns to the Christian community as a whole—understanding it to be composed of believers with different gifts.

12:3 everyone among you. The truth about spiritual gifts applies to each believer. **think sensibly.** The command is to know oneself (especially one's gifts) accurately, rather than to have too high an opinion of oneself in comparison to others. This attitude enables a body of believers to blend their gifts together in harmonious ministry.

12:4–5 Using a picture that could be understood in all cultures—the body—Paul defines the nature of the Christian community: diverse gifts, but all part of one body, the body of Christ.

12:5 members of one another. This is the critical insight that makes for harmony in the church. Believers must recognize that they are interdependent, needing to give to and receive from one another.

12:6 gifts. Those endowments given by God to every believer by grace (the words "grace" and "gifts" come from the same root word) to be used in God's service. The gifts listed here (or elsewhere) are not meant to be exhaustive or absolute since no gift list overlaps completely. **prophecy.** Inspired utterances, distinguished from teaching by their immediacy and unpremeditated nature, the source of which is direct revelation by God. Prophesying was highly valued in the New Testament church (1 Cor. 14:1). **according to the standard of faith.** This could mean that prophets are to resist adding their own words to the prophecy, or it could mean that they must measure their utterances in accord with "the faith"; i.e., Christian doctrine.

12:7 service. The capacity for rendering practical service to the needy. **teaching.** In contrast to the prophet (whose utterances have as their source the direct revelation of God), the teacher relied on the Old Testament Scriptures and the teachings of Jesus to instruct others.

12:8 Paul concludes his brief discussion of spiritual gifts with this emphasis on the fact that whatever gift one has, it should be exercised with enthusiasm for the good of others. **exhortation**. This is supporting and assisting others to live a life of obedience to God. **giving**. The person who takes delight in giving away his or her possessions. **leading**. Those with special ability to guide a congregation are called upon to do so with zeal. **showing mercy.** Those who help others in their afflictions. Note that three of the seven gifts involve practical assistance to the needy.

SESSION 4

DEVELOPING OUR GIFTS

SCRIPTURE: 1 CORINTHIANS 12:4-31

In last week's session, we focused on the topic of spiritual gifts and talked about discovering our own gifts. Today we will explore the subject further as we discuss how the gifts can and should be used to serve God.

ICE-BREAKER   Connect with your Group | 15 Min.

***LEADER**

Choose one, two or all three of the Ice-Breaker questions. Welcome and introduce new group members.

In this section, Paul uses the workings of the human body as an illustration of how the church works. Take time to get to know the other "body parts" in your group as you answer the following questions.

1. Which parts of the body do you identify with the most?
   - ○ A foot: I'll go anywhere to serve God.
   - ○ The hands: I like to help out.
   - ○ An ear: I am a good listener.
   - ○ The eyes: I can see what needs to be done.
   - ○ The head: I love to collect and impart knowledge of spiritual things.
   - ○ The mouth: I express myself well.
   - ○ Other_____.

2. When have you been pressed into some kind of volunteer work? Did you enjoy it?

3. When you were a child, what characteristic did you most want to change about yourself? What is your perspective on this now as an adult?

 **BIBLE STUDY** *Read Scripture and Discuss* | **30 Min.**

Paul wrote the following passage because some Christians at Corinth apparently felt that everyone should be the same and have the same gift. This attitude was causing division in the church. So Paul wrote to tell them that no gifts are inferior and that all are necessary in the body of Christ. Read 1 Corinthians 12:4–31 and think about what your own place is in the body.

A Variety of Gifts

Reader One: *⁴Now there are different gifts, but the same Spirit. ⁵There are different ministries, but the same Lord. ⁶And there are different activities, but the same God is active in everyone and everything. ⁷A manifestation of the Spirit is given to each person to produce what is beneficial:*

Reader Two: *⁸to one is given a message of wisdom through the Spirit,*

Reader One: *to another, a message of knowledge by the same Spirit,*

Reader Two: *⁹to another, faith by the same Spirit,*

Reader One: *to another, gifts of healing by the one Spirit,*

Reader Two: *¹⁰to another, the performing of miracles,*

Reader One: *to another, prophecy,*

Reader Two: *to another, distinguishing between spirits,*

Reader One: *to another, different kinds of languages,*

Reader Two: *to another, interpretation of languages.*

¹¹But one and the same Spirit is active in all these, distributing to each one as He wills.

Reader One: *¹²For as the body is one and has many parts, and all the parts of that body, though many, are one body—so also is Christ. ¹³For we were all bap-*

tized by one Spirit into one body—whether Jews or Greeks, whether slaves or free—and we were all made to drink of one Spirit.

Reader Two: *¹⁴So the body is not one part but many. ¹⁵If the foot should say, "Because I'm not a hand, I don't belong to the body," in spite of this it still belongs to the body. ¹⁶And if the ear should say, "Because I'm not an eye, I don't belong to the body," in spite of this it still belongs to the body. ¹⁷If the whole body were an eye, where would the hearing be? If the whole were an ear, where would be the sense of smell? ¹⁸But now God has placed the parts, each one of them, in the body just as He wanted. ¹⁹And if they were all the same part, where would the body be? ²⁰Now there are many parts, yet one body.*

Reader One: *²¹So the eye cannot say to the hand, "I don't need you!" nor again the head to the feet, "I don't need you!" ²²On the contrary, all the more, those parts of the body that seem to be weaker are necessary. ²³And those parts of the body that we think to be less honorable, we clothe these with greater honor, and our unpresentable parts have a better presentation. ²⁴But our presentable parts have no need of clothing. Instead, God has put the body together, giving greater honor to the less honorable, ²⁵so that there would be no division in the body, but that the members would have the same concern for each other. ²⁶So if one member suffers, all the members suffer with it; if one member is honored, all the members rejoice with it.*

Reader Two: *²⁷Now you are the body of Christ, and individual members of it. ²⁸And God has placed these in the church:*

Reader One: *first apostles, second prophets, third teachers, next, miracles, then gifts of healing, helping, managing, various kinds of languages.*

> *²⁹Are all apostles?*
> *Are all prophets?*
> *Are all teachers?*
> *Do all do miracles?*
> *³⁰Do all have gifts of healing?*
> *Do all speak in languages?*
> *Do all interpret?*

Reader Two: *³¹But desire the greater gifts. And I will show you an even better way.*

1 Corinthians 12:4–31

QUESTIONS FOR INTERACTION

***LEADER

Refer to the Summary and Study Notes at the end of this session as needed. If 30 minutes is not enough time to answer all of the questions in this section, conclude the Bible Study by answering question 7.

1. When have you been part of a team where everyone worked together as a unit for the common goal?

2. What attitudes have you encountered toward spiritual gifts and the question of their purpose and who receives them?

    ○ They are for ministers only.

    ○ They are for religious fanatics.

    ○ Those who are spiritually mature have them.

    ○ All believers receive gifts.

    ○ Gifts were for the first-century church only.

    ○ Only believers who have had a special experience receive gifts.

    ○ Other_____.

    What is your perspective?

3. Verses 4–6 indicate that some of the Corinthians felt certain spiritual gifts were better than others. Have you ever encountered that attitude among Christians? What about in yourself?

4. What happens in the human body when one organ takes over (such as the thyroid gland), or one organ malfunctions (such as the liver)? How does this illustration apply to the use of gifts in the church?

5. In the church in Corinth, what has happened to the people who have the supporting "weaker … less honorable" gifts (vv. 21–23)? What should the attitude be toward these people (vv. 24–26)? What is your church doing to "honor" and affirm the people with the supporting gifts?

6. How does this passage affect what you think about your place in the body of Christ, and your need for others?

7. How do you (or could you) use your gifts within the church, Christ's body? What holds you back from using your gifts more fully?

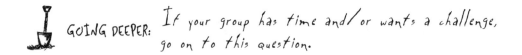

8. What is the "even better way" Paul refers to in verse 31? Read 1 Corinthians 13 and discuss how love affects the use of the gifts.

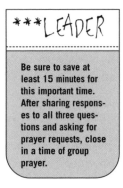

CARING TIME *Apply the Lesson & Pray for One another* | **15 Min.**

***LEADER**

Be sure to save at least 15 minutes for this important time. After sharing responses to all three questions and asking for prayer requests, close in a time of group prayer.

Take this time now to encourage and build up one another as members of the same body of Christ. Thank God for the gifts of the members of the group, and pray for God's guidance in using those gifts in a way that pleases him.

1. Who in your life has been a help to you in discovering and learning to use your spiritual gifts? How has someone else's gift been used to encourage or build you up?

2. How can this group pray for release from the things you mentioned in question 7 that you feel hold you back from using your gifts in the body?

3. In what ways have you seen God working through others in this group? What gifts do you think you see in each of their lives?

Today we further discussed the topic of spiritual gifts as we considered the special place each of us has in the body of Christ, and how we can use our gifts to best serve the body. This week, thank God for this special place he has given you (even if it does not seem very important or noticed), and ask him to help you to use your spiritual gifts with wisdom, love and humility. Next week we will continue to explore using our gifts as we talk about Jesus' parable of the talents and the risks and joys of investing in God's work.

NOTES ON 1 CORINTHIANS 12:4–31

Summary: In chapters 12-14 of I Corinthians, Paul is dealing with the third and final issue related to the worship experience of the Corinthian church: the abuse of the gift of tongues. His emphasis here is on the variety of gifts given by the Spirit, in contrast to the Corinthians' preoccupation with one particular gift.

12:5 ministries. The purpose of the gifts is to serve and aid others in various ways, yet all is done in the name of and for the sake of the same Lord.

12:6 activities. The Greek root is *energeia* ("energy"), and refers to the various ways in which God's power is displayed in the gifts.

12:7 to each person. Every Christian has a spiritual gift. **beneficial**. For the common good. The purpose of these gifts is not private advantage, but community growth.

12:8 wisdom / knowledge. It is not clear how (or if) these gifts differ. Perhaps a message of wisdom focused on practical, ethical instruction, while a message of knowledge involved exposition of biblical truth.

12:9 faith. Saving faith, which all Christians share, is not in view here. **healing**. Special ability to effect miraculous cures. Paul apparently had this gift (Acts 14:8–10).

12:10 performing of miracles. Possibly the gift of exorcism and similar types of confrontation with evil supernatural powers. **prophecy**. Inspired utterances given in ordinary (not ecstatic) speech, distinguished from teaching and wisdom by its unpremeditated nature. **distinguishing between spirits.** Just because a person claimed to be inspired by the Holy Spirit did not make it true. Those who possessed this gift of discernment were able to identify the source of an utterance—whether it came from the Holy Spirit or another spirit.

12:12–27 Having pointed out the diversity of gifts in 12:1–11, now Paul examines the unity that exists within all this diversity. Once having established that Christians are all part of one body (vv. 12–13), Paul returns then to the idea of diversity, in which he not only points out the variety of gifts that exist, but the fact that none are inferior and all are necessary.

12:12 the body is one and has many parts. This is Paul's central point in verses 12-30: "diversity within unity." So it is with Christ. The church is the body of Christ (v. 27), and so indeed Christ is understood to be made up of many parts. Yet he is also the Lord (12:3), and thus head over that church.

12:15–26 Having established that all Christians are part of one body (which is, in fact, Christ's body) and that this body has a variety of parts, Paul then develops an elaborate metaphor based on the human body. He makes two points: There are a variety of gifts (vv. 15–20), and each gift is vital, regardless of its nature (vv. 21–26).

12:15–20 It is just as ludicrous for Christians to opt out of the body of Christ (presumably by not using their gifts during worship) because they have one gift and not another (presumably more desirable gift), as it is for a foot (or an ear) to decide not to be a part of a physical body because it is not a hand (or an eye).

12:21–26 Just as it is presumptuous of the eye (or head) to say to the hand (or foot) that it has no need of it, so too, a Christian ought not to deny the value, need or function of anyone's spiritual gift, especially on the basis that it is different from (or inferior to) one's own gift.

12:21 Each part of the body needs the other parts. No one gift (e.g., tongues) can stand alone. Wholeness in the body requires that all the parts function together.

12:26 In fact, the whole person suffers when one (to use a modern example) sprains an ankle. It is not just the ankle that suffers.

12:27 the body of Christ. By this phrase, Paul conveys the idea not that Christ consists of this body, but that Christ rules over this body, and that this body belongs to him.

12:28 Paul offers a second list of the types of gifts given by the Holy Spirit (see the parallel list in Eph. 4:11)—mixing together ministries (apostles) with spiritual gifts (the gift of healing). **apostles**. These individuals were responsible for founding new churches. They were pioneer church planters. **prophets**. Those who were inspired to speak God's word to the church, in plain (not ecstatic) language. **teachers**. Those gifted to instruct others in the meaning of the Christian faith and its implication for one's life. **then**. Having first focused on those gifts whereby the church is established and nurtured, Paul then shifts to other gifts. **helping**. The gift of support; those whose function it was to aid the needy (e.g. the poor, the widow, the orphan). **managing**. The gift of direction (literally, the process of steering a ship through the rocks and safely to shore); those whose function it was to guide church affairs. **various kinds of languages**. This has come to mean ecstatic languages that require interpretation, although in Acts 2 these were the known languages of the Roman Empire.

SESSION 5

TAKING RISKS

SCRIPTURE: MATTHEW 25:14–30

LAST WEEK

In the session last week, we continued the discussion of spiritual gifts, focusing on the place each of us has in the body of Christ and the important truth that none of the gifts are inferior to others, even if they are not as noticeable. Today we are going to take a look at the concept of investing wholeheartedly in God's work.

ICE-BREAKER   Connect with your Group | 15 Min.

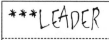

LEADER

Choose one or two of the Ice-Breaker questions. If you have a new group member, you may want to do all three. Remember to stick closely to the three-part agenda and the time allowed for each segment.

A certain amount of risk-taking is involved in all of our lives, just because we do not know the future. Take turns sharing from your own experiences with taking risks.

1. What kind of Monopoly player do you usually tend to be?
   ○ I play it safe and stash my cash.
   ○ I play on the edge of the cliff and gamble everything.
   ○ I stay cool and don't take too many risks.
   ○ Other_____.

2. What is the strangest foreign food you have ever tried? Did you like it? How do you feel about trying new foods?

3. What risky sport would you be most likely to try out?
   ○ Skydiving.
   ○ Underwater spelunking.
   ○ Swimming in the same river with an alligator.
   ○ Other _____.

46

It would be nice if God would just send us a heavenly telegram telling us exactly what our gifts and calling are. That way we could get to work without wondering whether we are doing what he wants us to be doing. But that isn't the way he works. Instead, finding and following our calling, whether in our career or in our role in the body of Christ, involves taking risks. Read Matthew 25:14–30 and listen to what Jesus has to say about investing in the kingdom of heaven.

The Parable of the Talents

¹⁴*"For it is just like a man going on a journey. He called his own slaves and turned over his possessions to them. ¹⁵To one he gave five talents; to another, two; and to another, one— to each according to his own ability. Then he went on a journey. Immediately ¹⁶the man who had received five talents went, put them to work, and earned five more. ¹⁷In the same way the man with two earned two more. ¹⁸But the man who had received one talent went off, dug a hole in the ground, and hid his master's money.*

¹⁹*"After a long time the master of those slaves came and settled accounts with them. ²⁰The man who had received five talents approached, presented five more talents, and said, 'Master, you gave me five talents. Look, I've earned five more talents.'*

²¹*"His master said to him, 'Well done, good and faithful slave! You were faithful over a few things; I will put you in charge of many things. Enter your master's joy!'*

²²*"Then the man with two talents also approached. He said, 'Master, you gave me two talents. Look, I've earned two more talents.'*

²³*"His master said to him, 'Well done, good and faithful slave! You were faithful over a few things; I will put you in charge of many things. Enter your master's joy!'*

²⁴*"Then the man who had received one talent also approached and said, 'Master, I know you. You're a difficult man, reaping where you haven't sown and gathering where you haven't scattered seed. ²⁵So I was afraid and went off and hid your talent in the ground. Look, you have what is yours.'*

²⁶*"But his master replied to him, 'You evil, lazy slave! If you knew that I reap where I haven't sown and gather where I haven't scattered, ²⁷then you should have deposited my money with the bankers. And when I returned I would have received my money back with interest.*

²⁸*" 'So take the talent from him and give it to the one who has 10 talents. ²⁹For to everyone who has, more will be given, and he will have more than enough. But from the one who does not have, even what he has will be taken away from him. ³⁰And throw this good-for-nothing slave into the outer darkness. In that place there will be weeping and gnashing of teeth.'*

Matthew 25:14–30

QUESTIONS FOR INTERACTION

***LEADER

Refer to the Summary
and Study Notes at the
conclusion of this ses-
sion as needed. If 30
minutes is not enough
time to answer all of
the questions in this
section, conclude the
Bible Study by
answering questions 6
and 7.

1. In your day-to-day life, do you see yourself as a risk-taker, or are you more cautious and less willing to change?

2. How do you differentiate between healthy risk-taking and foolhardy risk-taking?

3. What do you see as the main purpose of this parable?

4. Why do you think the servant who was given one talent hid his money?
   ○ He was afraid of his master.
   ○ He was afraid to take risks.
   ○ He didn't know what to do.
   ○ He was lazy and irresponsible.
   ○ He resented the way the master made his money.

5. In what way does God give more to those who have (v. 29)? What does the parable mean when it says, "from the one who does not have, even what he has will be taken away from him"?

6. What motivates you to use your time, resources and abilities for God's kingdom?
   ○ Fear of the Master.
   ○ The appreciation others show.
   ○ God's approval.
   ○ The desire for greater responsibility.
   ○ Fellowship with the Master.
   ○ Rewards in the next life.
   ○ Other_____.

7. How do you feel about the way you are currently investing your life? What changes would be necessary in order for you to be more satisfied with your life's investment?

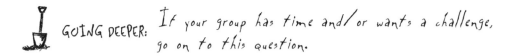 GOING DEEPER: *If your group has time and/or wants a challenge, go on to this question.*

8. At the end of the parable, the worthless servant is thrown outside and his talent is given to the slave who had ten. While this is a parable, and therefore not an exact parallel of reality, it all has some application. We are assured that our salvation does not rest on our own good works, but obviously there will be consequences for neglecting to use what God has given us. What are these consequences, and what should be our motivation for serving God?

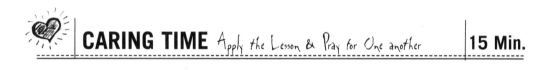 **CARING TIME** Apply the Lesson & Pray for One another | **15 Min.**

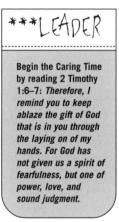

Begin the Caring Time by reading 2 Timothy 1:6–7: *Therefore, I remind you to keep ablaze the gift of God that is in you through the laying on of my hands. For God has not given us a spirit of fearfulness, but one of power, love, and sound judgment.*

It takes strength to be willing to take risks in our spiritual investments, and this is a good time to find some of the encouragement we need. Lift one another up as you pray and share together.

1. What is one area where you really feel the need for the spirit of "power, love, and sound judgment" as you seek to invest in God's kingdom?

2. In what area do you think God might be calling you to greater risks as you serve him? How can this group pray for you?

3. How can this group encourage you in your life right now?

NEXT WEEK

Today we explored the idea of investing our lives and gifts into God's kingdom, and looked at our own level of willingness to take risks with our lives. During the coming week, examine your own heart, and ask God to show you where you might be holding back from investing in him the way he means for you to. Ask him to help you overcome any fearfulness you may have and to be able to discern what he wants you to do. Next week we will continue to think about the "sins of omission" (burying our talents) and about how we should look at planning for the future.

NOTES ON MATTHEW 25:14–30

Summary: This parable (similar to that in Luke 19:11–27) is one of many Jesus told to clarify our role in doing the work of the kingdom of God. It underscores three points: (1) Christ's kingdom will not be established at this time; (2) Discipleship means faithful service to God while awaiting Christ's return; (3) Judgment awaits those who fail to invest themselves in the work of the kingdom. The term "talent" was first used as a monetary unit. The present-day use of the word to denote an ability or natural propensity most probably originates with this parable.

25:14 He called his own slaves and turned over his possessions to them. Wealthy people who had to travel on business would entrust their resources to capable servants who would act as managers of the estate in their absence. Their responsibility was to look after their master's interests in his absence, investing his resources in a way that would earn more money for him.

25:15 talents. Originally this was a unit of weight. However, it was also used as the highest denomination of coinage. It would take a laborer almost 20 years to earn the equivalent of one talent. **each according to his own ability.** The master took into account the level of responsibility he believed each servant could handle. Jesus is thus acknowledging that everyone does not start out at the same place in life. Some are given more in terms of abilities and possessions. But the rest of the parable reminds us that what matters is not what you are given, but how you make use of it.

25:16–18 As today, investing money always carried with it the risk that one might lose it. Yet two of the servants are reported as having had very good returns on their investments. The third servant, however, failed to do anything constructive with the money he was given to manage.

25:16 earned five more. High interest rates in that time could make a thousand percent return possible (though undoubtedly difficult).

25:18 dug a hole in the ground, and hid his master's money. In the absence of safe deposit boxes, this was a common way to protect money. However, its investment possibilities were nil! It was the low-risk option (there are no "no-risk" options—someone could have found it or he may have forgotten where he buried it, as implied in the parable of the hidden treasure in 13:44).

25:19 After a long time. The indefinite time reference hints that Christ's own return may be far off. After Jesus ascended to heaven, much of the church was expecting his early return (Heb. 10:37; 1 Peter 4:7; Rev. 1:3). When this did not happen, they had to be taught how to wait. Parables such as this helped, as did teaching such as 1 Thessalonians 4:13–18 and 2 Peter 3:3–10. **settled accounts.** This was the time of reckoning, in which the master would evaluate how the various servants had fulfilled their responsibility to him.

25:20 Look. The emphasis here is on the fact that the servant welcomes the master's inspection because he knows he has done a good job. For him, this inspection is not a fearful time.

25:21 Well done, good and faithful slave! The servant's faithfulness in this matter is the quality that allows the master to trust him with greater responsibility. The second servant is given the same commendation and type of reward (vv. 22–23). **few things / many things.** The servant is rewarded, not with a life of ease, but with greater administrative responsibility in the master's household (based on the master's trust and confidence in him). While five talents or even two talents is by no means a small amount, the point is that they are "a few things" in comparison with the responsibility with which these servants will now be entrusted. **Enter your master's joy.** The servants are not only given more responsibility; they are invited into a new relationship with the master. No longer simply slaves, they now enjoy his friendship and respect. Jesus spoke of this same change in relationship in John 15:15 when he told the disciples, "I no longer call you servants, because a servant does not know his master's business. Instead, I have called you friends."

25:24–25 In contrast to the other two, this servant had simply hidden the money away where it did no good. The servant's reasoning for doing so was based on his fear of failing to live up to the master's high expectations. He assumed it would be better to safely return the money rather than risk having to make up any loss he may have incurred by making a bad investment.

25:24 a difficult man. Literally, this is "exacting." The description of the master is uncomplimentary; it pictures him as ruthless, harvesting for himself the fruits for which other people have worked. While the inclinations of the listeners (who were poor) might naturally lead them to favor the slave over a "hard" rich man, nothing in the story so far indicates that the servant's characterization of the master was correct. He was generous in his original entrustment of his property to his servants. He was generous to the first and second servants upon his return. It would raise the question in the listeners' minds whether the problem was with the third servant's perceptions.

25:25 So I was afraid. The servant implies that his lack of having anything to show for having been entrusted with the talent is really the fault of the master: He expects too much and he is too frightening. **Look, you have what is yours.** Rabbinic teaching emphasized that God had given Israel the responsibility to protect the Law until the time came when he would establish his kingdom. Considering that this parable occurs just prior to Jesus' death, it may be that Jesus has this tradition in mind with this parable. While the Pharisees have "protected" the Law from being corrupted by the masses, they have failed to use it in a way that would draw others to God. They can only return it to God intact, but without being able to show any benefit from having been entrusted with it. Thus, their judgment is assured. His disciples are to do better than that.

25:26 You evil, lazy slave! This may seem harsh, since when we really look at what the servant did, many would say it was not so bad. He did not embezzle the money or use it for his own ends. He just played it safe. That can certainly be seen as being "lazy," but was it "evil"? Here is where parables must not be forced into being exact parallels of the situation to which they are addressed. The master, while not as harsh as the servant pictured, is at least rather materially focused and stricter than the New Testament pictures God to be. However, when we look at what the parable was teaching, neglecting to properly use the talents and gifts God has given is both lazy and evil, because it is an abuse of God's gift. Even more specifically, Jesus may have had in mind the special entrustment God had given to Israel of his Word. Instead of multiplying it and spreading it to other people and other nations, they "hid it in the ground" and kept it to themselves.

25:27 deposited. Literally, the phrase here is "on the table." The table used by money changers in Jerusalem is in view. To invest the money with these money changers guaranteed a high rate of return. The parable is not meant to condone this practice. The story simply uses this practice as a fact of life the hearers would have understood.

25:28–30 Judgment is pronounced upon this servant. The faithless servant loses the capital he had been given, while it is added to the interest of the most faithful servant. By doing so, the master shows that the faithless servant's characterization of him as hard and miserly is false. The point of this part of the parable is to warn the disciples to apply themselves to the task of serving Jesus with all diligence. God expects those to whom he has entrusted various gifts to be faithful and diligent in their use of them for his purposes.

25:29 everyone who has ... the one who does not have. The judgment is justified by use of a common saying found in other New Testament contexts as well (13:12; Mark 4:25; Luke 8:18). The saying illustrates a spiritual principle about discipleship that has many implications: Those who hear and prac-tice the word from God that they have been given are those who will be able to understand and receive more from God. Those who neglect what they have already heard will not be given any more.

25:30 throw this good-for-nothing slave into the outer darkness. In that place there will be weeping and gnash-ing of teeth. This is a graphic, stock phrase often used to express the sever-ity of God's judgment (8:12; 13:42,50; 22:13; 24:51; Luke 13:28).

SESSION 6

WHO OWNS THE FUTURE?

SCRIPTURE: JAMES 4:13–17

LAST WEEK

Last week's session focused on spiritual investing, and we talked about taking risks for God as we studied the parable of the talents. This week we will continue our discussion of the sin of "burying your talent," and also talk about how we should look at planning for the future with God's will in mind.

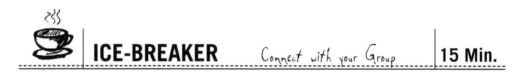

ICE-BREAKER
Connect with your Group
15 Min.

***LEADER**

Begin the session with a word of prayer, asking God for his blessing and presence. Choose, one, two or all three Ice-Breaker questions, depending on your group's needs.

Some of us plan ahead more than others. Share with one another now from your own experiences by taking turns answering the following questions.

1. When you were 14, what did you think you would be doing at 24? How close to the truth were you?

2. When you travel, how much planning do you do?
   ○ I am still looking for my passport three hours before my international flight.
   ○ I always have everything arranged down to the minute details.
   ○ I try to plan ahead, but I'm flexible with last-minute alterations.
   ○ I like to be a free spirit.
   ○ I don't even know whether I'm going until I actually leave.
   ○ Other_____.

3. When has some unexpected event forced you to make a drastic change in your plans?

**LEADER**

Select a member of the group ahead of time to read aloud the passage. Then discuss the Questions for Interaction, dividing into subgroups of three to six.

The book of James is known for its direct, even blunt, exhortations about living out the Christian faith. In this passage, James is challenging Christians to rethink the way they look at planning for the future and making money. Read James 4:13–17 and reflect on your own attitudes, especially noticing the last verse.

Boasting About Tomorrow

¹³*Come now, you who say, "Today or tomorrow we will travel to such and such a city and spend a year there and do business and make a profit."* ¹⁴*You don't even know what tomorrow will bring—what your life will be! For you are a bit of smoke that appears for a little while, then vanishes.*

¹⁵*Instead, you should say, "If the Lord wills, we will live and do this or that."* ¹⁶*But as it is, you boast in your arrogance. All such boasting is evil.* ¹⁷*So, for the person who knows to do good and doesn't do it, it is a sin.*

James 4:13-17

 **QUESTIONS FOR INTERACTION**

LEADER

Refer to the Summary and Study Notes at the end of this session as needed. If 30 minutes is not enough time to answer all of the questions in this section, conclude the Bible Study by answering questions 6 and 7.

1. How far into the future have you planned your life?

2. How seriously do you tend to take your own plans for your life?
   ○ Not at all—I just make plans so I won't stagnate.
   ○ I have a really hard time being flexible.
   ○ I don't take no for an answer and push for my goals.
   ○ I don't make plans—I'd rather just drift.
   ○ I try to make my plans with my heart open to having them changed by God's leading.
   ○ Other _____.

3. What is wrong with the kind of planning James talks about in verses 13 and 14? What would happen in your life if you made no plans at all?

4. How easy is it for you to have the outlook James calls for in verse 15?
   ○ I don't know if I can relax enough.
   ○ I don't think that it is responsible.
   ○ It is hard, but I will try.
   ○ I don't have enough experience trusting God.
   ○ I have learned how.
   ○ It is the only way to go.
   ○ Other _____.

5. What is the boasting James is rebuking? In what ways do you think you may have fallen into this habit in your own life?

6. Take a moment to reflect on how verse 17 is true for your life, particularly when it comes to your work and career planning. When have you "buried your talent" and failed to do the good that you could have done? What is usually the reason you don't do what you know you should?

7. What does this passage say to you about the plans you are making for your future? Where do you need God's guidance?

GOING DEEPER: *If your group has time and/or wants a challenge, go on to this question.*

8. We often struggle with guilt over failing to meet other people's expectations, but sometimes this guilt is false guilt rather than true moral guilt. How do you tell the difference between what God wants you to do, your own natural inclinations and what other people think you should do?

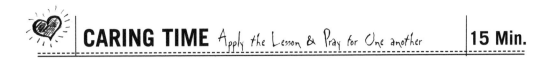

CARING TIME *Apply the Lesson & Pray for One another* | 15 Min.

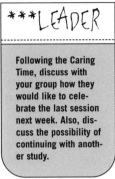

***LEADER

Following the Caring Time, discuss with your group how they would like to celebrate the last session next week. Also, discuss the possibility of continuing with another study.

Recognizing that God has the ultimate say in what happens to us in the future is actually a freeing realization. It is a relief to know that someone wiser and stronger is in control. Take this time now to thank him for his care and guidance.

1. What future plans do you have that you need to release to God's leadership and guidance? Does releasing "ownership" of your future seem scary?

2. For what situation in your life would you like prayer as you seek to plan ahead with God's will in mind?

3. What special requests or praises would you like to share with the group before we close in prayer?

NEXT WEEK

Today we focused on releasing ownership of our future into God's hands, and continued the discussion of last week as we thought about the "sins of omission." In the coming week, ask God to help you trust him with your future, and also ask him to point out areas of your life where you are neglecting to do the good you know you should. Ask him to help you to change in these areas. Next week we will conclude this study by discussing what it means to be a servant.

Summary: In verses 13-17, James begins discussion of his third and final theme: testing. He will deal with this theme, at first, as it touches the issue of wealth. He has just spoken about a particular form of disharmony within the Christian community, that which is generated by slander and judgment (4:11-12). The problem is the difficulty that comes with being wealthy and the tensions this brings, both on a personal level and for the whole community. In this first part of his discussion, he looks at the situation of a group of Christian businessmen—in particular, at their "sins of omission."

4:13 Boasting about what will happen tomorrow is another example of human arrogance. It is in the same category as judging one another. Judgment is arrogant because God is the only legitimate judge. Boasting about the future is arrogant because God is the only one who knows what will happen in the future. Such arrogance is the opposite of humility, which is supposed to characterize Christians. **Come now.** This comment stands in sharp contrast to the way James has been addressing his readers. In the previous section he called them "my brothers" (3:1,10,12). James reverts to more impersonal language in addressing these merchants. **Today or tomorrow we will travel.** James lets us listen in on the plans of a group of businessmen. Possibly they are looking at a map together. In any case, they are planning for the future and are concerned with where they will go, how long they will stay, what they will do and how much profit they will make. It appears to be an innocent conversation, the kind of conversation anyone in trade might have. But that is part of the problem: James is saying that a Christian should look at these things differently than a non-Christian. **we will travel.** Travel by traders in the first century usually took

the form of caravan or ship. There were no hard and fast timetables. Instead, one had to wait until the right transportation came along going in your direction. However, there were certain seasons when ships sailed and caravans were more likely to travel. **do business.** The word James uses here is derived from the Greek word *emporos*, from which the English word "emporium" comes. It denotes wholesale merchants who traveled from city to city, buying and selling. A different word was used to describe local peddlers who had small businesses in the bazaars. The growth of cities and the increase of trade during the Greco-Roman era created great opportunities for making money. In the Bible a certain distrust of traders is sometimes expressed (Prov. 20:23; Amos 8:4–6; Rev. 18:11–20).

4:14 tomorrow. All such planning presupposes that tomorrow will unfold like any other day, when in fact, the future is anything but secure (Prov. 27:1). **what your life will be!** Is it not death that is the great unknown? Who can know when death will come and interrupt plans? Jesus' parable of the rich farmer in Luke 12:16-21 illustrates the same problem. Christians need to realize that their security comes from God, not from material considerations or their own knowledge of the future. **bit of smoke.** Hosea 13:3 says, "Therefore they will be like the morning mist, like the early dew that disappears, like chaff swirling from a threshing floor, like smoke escaping through a window" (NIV).

4:15 If the Lord wills. This phrase (often abbreviated D.V. after its Latin form) is not used in the Old Testament, though it was found frequently in Greek and Roman literature and is used by Paul (Acts 18:21; 1 Cor. 4:19; 16:7). The uncertainty of the future ought not to be a terror to the Christian. Instead, it ought to force on him or her awareness of how dependent a person is upon God, and thus move that person to a planning that involves God. **we will live and do this or that.** James is not ruling out planning. He says plan, but keep God in mind.

4:16 In contrast to such prayerful planning, these Christian merchants are very proud of what they do on their own. James is not condemning international trade as such, nor the wealth it produced. (His comments on riches come in 5:1–6.) What he is concerned about is that all this is done without reference to God, in a spirit of boastful arrogance. **boast**. The problem with this boasting is that they are claiming to have the future under control when, in fact, it is God who holds time in his hands. These are empty claims.

4:17 Some feel that this proverb-like statement may, in fact, be a saying of Jesus that did not get recorded in the Gospel accounts. In any case, by it James points out the nature of so-called "sins of omission." In other words, it is sin when we fail to do what we ought to do. The more familiar definition is of "sins of commission" or wrongdoing (1 John 3:4). In other words, sinning can be both active and passive. Christians can sin by doing what they ought not to do (law-breaking); or by not doing what they know they should do (failure). **who knows to do good.** James applies this principle to the merchants. It is not that they are cheating and stealing in the course of their business (that would be active wrongdoing). The problem is in what they fail to do. Generally James defines "the good" as acts of charity toward those in need. And certainly in the context of this letter, it would appear that these men are failing in their duty to the poor. Rather than spending all our energy in earthly investments, Jesus told us to invest in heaven (Matt. 6:19-21).

SESSION 7

HAVING A SERVANT MIND

SCRIPTURE: JOHN 13:1-17

In last week's session, we talked about releasing "ownership" of our future into God's hands (where it really is, whether we like it or not). In this final session, we will focus on having a servant attitude as we seek to do God's will.

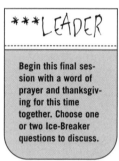

ICE-BREAKER   Connect with your Group | 15 Min.

***LEADER**

Begin this final session with a word of prayer and thanksgiving for this time together. Choose one or two Ice-Breaker questions to discuss.

Nearly everyone has probably wished for a personal servant at some point. Share your answers to the following questions about service.

1. If you could have one servant to do part of your work, what kind of servant would you want?
   ○ An elegant English butler.
   ○ A personal slave who would rub my back and bring me coffee.
   ○ A scullery maid, so I would never have to wash dishes.
   ○ A valet who would keep my clothes perfectly in order.
   ○ A hired man to do the heavy work around the house.
   ○ Other_____.

2. Where did you receive the best service at a hotel or restaurant? Where was the service the lousiest?

3. Do you like full-service stations, or do you prefer to pump your own gas?

***LEADER**

Select three members of the group ahead of time to read aloud the Scripture passage. Have one member read John's narration; another read the part of Jesus; and the other read the part of Peter. Then discuss the Questions for Interaction, dividing into subgroups of three to six.

As we have learned in the previous lessons, God expects us to use the gifts we have been given for his glory; we sin when we fail to do good. But doing good grudgingly or out of fear is not God's plan, either. Instead, he is looking for willing servants, eager to do his will. He wants the kind of servants who will do more than they have been asked, just for love of him. Read John 13:1-17 and see the example Jesus himself gave us for the kind of self-giving service he expects.

Jesus Washes the Disciples Feet

John: 13 *Before the Passover Festival, Jesus knew that His hour had come to depart from this world to the Father. Having loved His own who were in the world, He loved them to the end. ²Now by the time of supper, the Devil had already put it into the heart of Judas, Simon Iscariot's son, to betray Him. ³Jesus knew that the Father had given everything into His hands, that He had come from God, and that He was going back to God. ⁴So He got up from supper, laid aside His robe, took a towel, and tied it around Himself. ⁵Next, He poured water into a basin and began to wash His disciples' feet and to dry them with the towel tied around Him. ⁶He came to Simon Peter, who asked Him,*

Peter: *"Lord, are You going to wash my feet?"*

Jesus: *⁷Jesus answered him, "What I'm doing you don't understand now, but afterward you will know."*

Peter: *⁸"You will never wash my feet—ever!" Peter said.*

Jesus: *Jesus replied, "If I don't wash you, you have no part with Me."*

Peter: *⁹Simon Peter said to Him, "Lord, not only my feet, but also my hands and my head."*

Jesus: *¹⁰"One who has bathed," Jesus told him, "doesn't need to wash anything except his feet, but he is completely clean. You are clean, but not all of you."*

John: *"For He knew who would betray Him. This is why He said, "You are not all clean." ¹²When Jesus had washed their feet and put on His robe, He reclined again and said to them,*

Jesus: *"Do you know what I have done for you? ¹³You call Me Teacher and Lord. This is well said, for I am. ¹⁴So if I, your Lord and Teacher, have washed your feet, you also ought to wash one another's feet. ¹⁵For I have given you an example that you also should do just as I have done for you. ¹⁶"I assure you: A slave is not greater than his master, and a messenger is not greater than the one who sent him. ¹⁷If you know these things, you are blessed if you do them.*

John 13:1-17

 ## QUESTIONS FOR INTERACTION

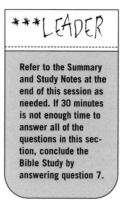

***LEADER

Refer to the Summary and Study Notes at the end of this session as needed. If 30 minutes is not enough time to answer all of the questions in this section, conclude the Bible Study by answering question 7.

1. When have you experienced an act of selfless service that encouraged and blessed you?

2. If you had been one of the disciples on this evening, how do you think you would have responded to Jesus washing your feet?

3. What do you do for your family right now that is most like "washing feet"—a somewhat unpleasant, humble servant-task? How do you feel about doing this?

4. How did Jesus love his disciples "to the end" (v. 1)? In what ways have you felt this love?

5. What is the significance of Jesus' statements in verses 8 and 10? Have you been "washed"?

6. Do you think the disciples understood Jesus' teaching on leadership? Do you think the church today understands leadership? Who in particular have you seen modeling "Jesus-style" leadership?

7. What is holding you back from living a life of service such as Jesus demonstrated and taught?
   ○ I'm afraid I'll be taken advantage of.
   ○ I don't have time.
   ○ I'm not willing to do things that aren't my job.
   ○ I guess I'm too selfish.
   ○ I don't know where to start.
   ○ Other _____.

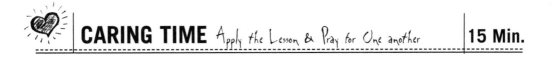

GOING DEEPER: *If your group has time and/or wants a challenge, go on to this question.*

8. What does Jesus mean in verse 17? How is a person blessed by being a servant and "foot washer"? When have you been blessed by serving others?

CARING TIME *Apply the Lesson & Pray for One another* | **15 Min.**

LEADER

Begin this final Caring Time by reading Philippians 2:5-11 to the group, which emphasizes Jesus' humility and willingness to serve. Conclude by praying for each group member and asking for God's blessing on any plans to start a new group or continue to study together.

The concept of being a servant is sometimes hard to grasp, but Jesus has given us an incredible example. Spend this time serving one another by listening to and praying for each other.

1. How can we in this group do a better job of loving and serving one another? How about in our church body? In our homes or workplaces? Pray for God's leadership and help as you seek to serve others.

2. What kind of encouragement from your fellow servants do you need in your life right now?

3. What will you remember most about this group? How would you like the group to continue to pray for you?

Summary: This passage describes an event during the Last Supper that Jesus celebrated with his disciples on the night before his death. It was customary for people's dusty, sandaled feet to be washed, usually by the lowest-ranking servant, before a meal was served. As an example of perfect servant-leadership, Jesus washed his disciples' feet himself, and then instructed them to treat each other with the same attitude of love and service.

13:1 Before the Passover Festival. This final week, begun in John 12:1, is approaching its end. In the other gospels, the Last Supper is the Passover meal itself with Jesus being killed on the following day. This gospel, however, emphasizes John's theological understanding of Jesus as the Lamb of God (John 1:29) **Jesus knew**. Here, in verse 3 and in verse 11, John emphasizes what Jesus knew. This lays stress on the fact that Jesus was in charge of the events leading to his death (John 10:18). In contrast to the crowds and to the authorities who did not know him (John 9:29), Jesus is fully aware of his identity and mission. This was in full awareness of his dignity and power that Jesus washed the disciples' feet (Phil. 2:5–11). **Having loved His own.** This is not to be taken exclusively, as if Jesus loved only those who were part of his elite club. Christ loves all who respond to his love and he sees them as his own. **who were in the world.** This gospel contrasts being in the world with being of the world (John 8:23; 9:39; 15:19; 17:11–18; 18:36–37). Being in the world is in some respects just a matter of location. However, it exposes the believer, who is in a sense a foreigner in a foreign land, to hostility. Being of the world means to have the world's values, as opposed to the values of God.

13:3 Jesus' self-knowledge was at the heart of his willingness and ability to serve. This verse says that he knew who he was in terms of where he had come from (God), where he was going (back to God), and what his role was while he was here. That kind of knowledge made him secure enough that serving others did not threaten his ego, as it does some people who do not know these things.

13:4–5 Normally people's dusty, sandaled feet were washed by the lowest-ranking servant of the household before a meal was served. Jesus' action was deliberate. Removing his outer clothing was a sign he was going to do some work, and it would have identified him with a servant who generally worked in minimal garb. The other gospels mention that at the Last Supper there was a discussion among the Twelve about who was the greatest (Luke 22:24), so this may have been the motive for Jesus' action. In that context, Jesus identified the greatest as the one who was the servant (Luke 22:25–26).

13:6 Lord, are You going to wash my feet? Peter, recognizing the impropriety of a master washing the servants' feet, protests. The Greek sentence actually reads more like, "You? Wash my feet?" Peter is appalled at this breach of normal procedure.

13:7 afterward you will know. This may simply be referring to verse 17, but more likely it refers to the full understanding of Jesus' servanthood that will be made clear after his resurrection. It also has significance in that it could be a theme for the disciples' entire relationship with Jesus up until the Resurrection. There was so much they didn't understand until looking back after Christ's resurrection and ascension (Mark 4:13; 6:51–52; 8:14–21; 9:30–32; John 12:16).

13:8 If I don't wash you, you have no part with Me. This lifts the meaning of the footwashing to a higher plane than simply that of an object lesson about humility. Although it could not be understood at the time, the image of being "cleansed" by Jesus became a common picture of what it meant to be forgiven of sin (1 John 1:7,9; Rev. 7:14). Jesus' footwashing was a symbol of the spiritual cleansing he would accomplish for his followers through the Cross.

13:10 One who has bathed. Jesus uses the picture of a person who, after washing completely, travels somewhere. Upon arrival, only his feet need be washed to be clean again. **You are clean, but not all of you.** The meaning is left somewhat ambiguous to the hearers. He may mean only that they are literally still not all clean, but the context shows his real intent was to prepare them for his startling announcement in verse 21.

13:13 Teacher and Lord. These titles of respect for a rabbi were commonly used of Jesus throughout this gospel (1:38; 13:6). Jesus acknowledges that they are appropriate to him; yet, just as he laid aside the pretension of these titles in order to love others, so they should follow his example in expressing love for one another.

13:16 A slave is not greater than his master. If the master serves, how much more should the servants do so? **a messenger.** This is the same word as "apostle," which only occurs here in this gospel. An apostle was a person sent with the authority to represent the one who sent him. Jesus' followers are to represent his servanthood to others.

PERSONAL NOTES

PERSONAL NOTES